Contents

Introduction

At some time or other we have all helped someone who is in trouble. Sometimes we may just listen to their problems, do a favour for them or give money to a charity. Throughout history people have helped those who are less fortunate than they are. In modern times richer countries have begun to help poorer countries, and this kind of assistance has come to be known as 'aid'.

An unequal world

Globalisation, in which countries are becoming more closely linked through the growth of trade and communications, has brought different cultures closer together and resulted in many benefits – but not for all. In a number of cases the benefits seem to have gone to those who already have a lot, while the poorest have become even poorer. While a few people

▲ A young beggar asks for money from holiday shoppers crowding New York's Fifth Avenue. Poverty exists in rich countries as well as those that are less economically developed.

▲ Following the 2004 Boxing Day tsunami a school is rebuilt in Sri Lanka with funding from Oxfam.

Our awareness of need

In an increasingly interdependent world, greater contact between people makes the widening gap between rich and poor appear more stark. We are all much more aware of what happens in other parts of the world and what suffering looks like. Many people are moved to respond to these shocking images and donate money to charities, or lobby their government to provide help. Some people even decide to go there and help directly, especially if they are nurses or doctors. But it is not only when disaster strikes that many countries need and receive help. Many countries are dependent on aid on a long-term basis. Aid is a huge global undertaking and a major feature of the relationship between rich and poor countries.

However, more and more questions are being asked about why aid is still necessary and what happens to all the money. Does it go to the people who are in most need? How is it spent? Does it make any difference? How can globalisation be made to work more effectively for poor people?

live with almost unimaginable wealth and some live in very comfortable circumstances, millions of people – one fifth of the world's population – live in poverty. Although the world is often divided into rich and poor countries, it is important to remember that there are also differences in wealth *within* countries as well as *between* them.

Whatever the reasons for the differences in wealth between countries, most people recognise that it is undesirable for there to be such inequality. This is partly for moral and humanitarian reasons – that it is simply wrong not to take action. It is also because this disparity can lead to political and economic instability, causing conflicts and wars that would benefit no one. However, some countries give aid to others purely to further their own interests.

Percentage of people living below the poverty line	
Region	Population below US$1 per day (%)
East Asia (including China)	27.58
East Asia (excluding China)	18.51
Eastern Europe and Central Asia	1.56
Latin America and Caribbean	6.80
Middle East and North Africa	2.39
South Asia	44.01
Sub-Saharan Africa	47.67
(Source: UNDP 2000)	

▲ This table shows the percentage of people living below the poverty line in the major regions of the world.

Global Poverty and Development

In this book the word 'aid' is used to mean the assistance that richer countries give to poorer countries. This is also known as 'foreign aid', 'international aid' and 'overseas aid'. It is given when a country is faced with a disaster, after a war or to help a country develop economically and socially.

The beginnings of aid and development

Perhaps the first large-scale aid programme was the Marshall Plan in 1947. This was not intended to help developing countries but was a huge programme of economic and social aid given by the United States to help Europe recover from the devastation of the Second World War. Up to US$20 billion was offered on condition that European countries got together and drew up a plan on how they would use the money. Although it was very generous, the programme also benefited the United States because much of the money was used to buy goods from the US.

Two years later, in 1949, US President Harry S. Truman said that the recent advances in industry and technology should be made available and shared with what he called the 'underdeveloped' areas. He was referring to countries in Africa and Asia, and he possibly had the success of the Marshall Plan in mind.

▼ American soldiers load up a plane with essential supplies during the Berlin Airlift (1948–49). Such supplies were airlifted into Berlin by American, French and British planes after Soviet forces surrounded and closed off the city.

AID AND DEVELOPMENT

Ali Brownlie Bojang

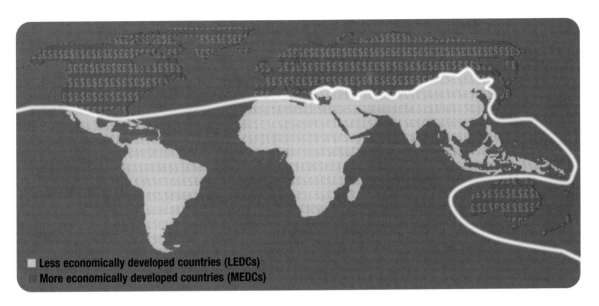

Less economically developed countries (LEDCs)
More economically developed countries (MEDCs)

▲ This map shows how the world is divided into 'North' and 'South'. Most countries in the north are considered more economically developed countries (MEDCs), while most of those in the south are LEDCs.

The success of the Marshall Plan has given some people the idea that a similar plan might work in Africa today.

Colonialism and trade

Until the middle of the twentieth century, Europe had benefited enormously from trading with its colonies and, although there were some benefits for the colonies in terms of new railways and ports, at independence they had been left without a fully working infrastructure and they were still dependent on their former European colonial powers for trade. Although many had the right conditions to be self-sufficient in food, the land had been given over to producing cash crops such as sugar and coffee. These countries were poor.

The world divides

In the 1960s, after most developing nations had become independent, the ex-colonial powers felt some responsibility towards their former colonies and, together with the

United States, began to react to what they saw as the threat of communism. They decided that they needed to have some influence on these countries. Many newly independent nations formed their own movement of 'non-aligned' countries, which meant that they did not support the West (the 'First World') or the communist world (the 'Second World'). They became known as the 'Third World'. Since then they have also been known as the 'South', 'less economically developed countries' (LEDCs), or the 'majority world'.

Eyewitness

'To those peoples in the huts and villages of half the globe struggling to break the bonds of mass misery, we pledge our best efforts to help them help themselves... If a free society cannot help the many who are poor, it can never serve the few who are rich.'
US President John F. Kennedy, at the launch of the United Nations Decade of Development, 1960

What is poverty?

Aid is usually – although not always – given to stop poverty. But what is poverty? It is not only about not having money. Poverty also exists when people's needs are not met. These needs can be for food, water and shelter but they can also be for self-esteem, companionship and happiness.

When people's basic needs are not met they are described as being in 'absolute poverty'. Another type of poverty is when people have less than those around them in society. This might be when they are not valued or are excluded by society. This kind of poverty is known as 'relative poverty'.

Does money make you happy?

A study in 2007 found that children in the richest countries were not necessarily the happiest. It revealed that among 20 other MEDCs, the United States and the United Kingdom were the worst places to be a child. The report looked at material well-being, health, education, relationships, behaviours and risks, and young people's own sense of happiness.

In Bhutan, a remote country in the Himalaya mountains, the happiness of the people is considered more important than how much money they have. Many of the measures taken by the government mean that people

▼ Will the children of Bhutan grow up to be happier without the trappings of wealth?

▲ Easy access to clean water is a basic need that millions of people do not have.
This child in Somalia is taking advantage of a tap provided by a development agency.

are actually less well-off than they could have been – but apparently they are happier.

This does not mean that money is not important. It is essential to provide basic needs and comforts, but it seems that beyond a certain amount, it does nothing to make people happier. However, many people in LEDCs lack even the most basic facilities, and after more than half a century of aid and development, many countries are still poor – in fact some are actually poorer.

What is development?

Development is a process of change and growth. It usually involves an improvement in people's lives so that they become better, happier and freer.

Many understand the idea of development mainly in economic terms, but it should also include social and human development, as well as issues such as respect for the environment, democracy and human rights. There are many different ideas and theories about development and how it should be carried out in ways that will improve people's lives. There are a number of different types or areas of development.

Eyewitness

'It was a shock to us to see the unemployed people of Easterhouse (Glasgow, UK) had cars and televisions and refrigerators – incredible wealth to many Indians – and yet they were apathetic and had no hope. Despite their possessions, they were worse off than the poorest tribesman.'
Stan and Mari Thekaekara, development workers from India describing relative poverty in Scotland

▲ Being able to read and write has been described as the human right that enables someone to pursue the other human rights to which they are entitled. Here, a farmer and his wife in Bolivia attend a literacy class – part of a national programme aimed at wiping out illiteracy in two and a half years.

Economic development

The majority of aid is given to help countries develop economically. Countries are assisted in building structures such as factories and dams, producing natural resources and providing services such as communications systems – for example mobile-phone networks – and hospitals. By making the country itself richer, it is believed that wealth will 'trickle down' and reduce the poverty of the people. Economic development does lead to increased per-capita income, but this statistic hides the fact that it is often only the rich who get richer while the poor either stay poor or get even poorer.

It is important to recognise that there are different kinds of aid and that one kind could be more effective than another. Aid that involves large projects and governments is particularly open to criticism, as the projects may be focused on economic development and do not necessarily benefit the lives of the poor. This kind of aid is also more open to corruption.

Social and human development

Social and human development works to help people improve the quality of their lives. It is usually focused on people rather than governments. People may be helped to read and write, provided with better healthcare or funded to set up businesses so they can earn their own living. Social development also works to ensure that people are more involved in improving their own communities. In recent years there has also been an emphasis on human rights.

Sustainable development

In 1987 the Brundtland Commission introduced the idea of sustainable development. This suggested that the environment will be damaged if economic development continues without giving thought to how it might affect the future. It emphasises the need to balance social development with the way in which the environment and economies develop, so that what happens now will not jeopardise the future. Sustainable development is now recognised as critical for the future of the planet.

Focus on...
Development through theatre

Many aid projects use theatre and drama to communicate information on a range of social and legal issues. This is particularly useful when people cannot read. Some dramas use puppets. Many dramas are aimed at women and focus on particular problems that they may face, such as basic hygiene practices and their legal rights. Women are often asked to participate in the dramas and come up with their own solutions to the problems presented. Using theatre is seen as a very entertaining and effective way of learning about and involving people in very serious issues of human development.

▼ Since the 1990s India has benefited enormously from economic development, but despite this the vast majority of its population still lives in poverty. These people are sifting through rubble to find rocks that can be reused for building.

The Millennium Development Goals

In September 2000, to mark the new millennium, world leaders at the United Nations Millennium Summit agreed to work together to fight against poverty, hunger, disease, illiteracy, environmental damage and discrimination against women. What they came up with became known as the Millennium Development Goals (MDGs). A target date of 2015 was set, by which time specific goals should be met. The UN also stated that it would 'spare no effort to free our fellow men, women and children from the abject and dehumanising conditions of extreme poverty to which more than a billion of them are currently subjected'.

The Millennium Development Goals are to:

● Halve extreme poverty and hunger
● Educate every child
● Provide equal chances for girls and women
● Reduce the number of babies and children under five who die
● Ensure safe and healthy motherhood
● Fight diseases, especially HIV/AIDS and malaria
● Ensure a clean and sustainable environment
● Share responsibility for making the world a better place by creating a global partnership to ensure fair aid, trade and debt relief

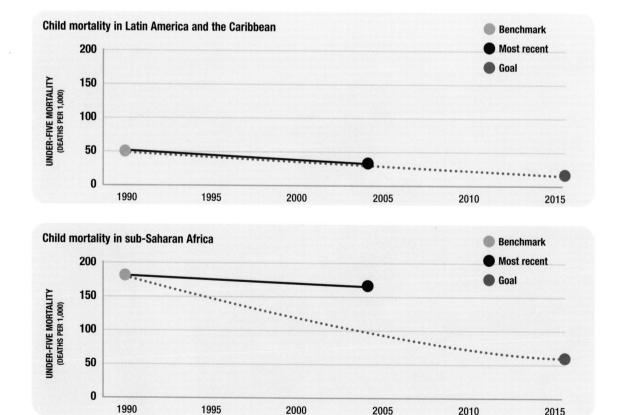

▲ Sub-Saharan Africa is far off meeting its goal of reducing under-five mortality, while Latin America and the Caribbean are on target.

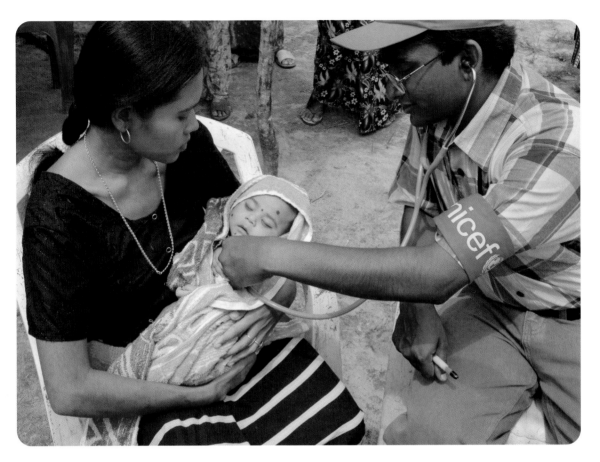

▲ Careful monitoring of infants and immunisation programmes play an important role in preventing child mortality. Here a child is being examined by a UNICEF doctor on Car Nicobar Island in the Bay of Bengal.

A global partnership

Every year progress on the goals is measured. For the first seven goals governments of LEDCs have the responsibility of ensuring that the targets are met or improved on. The eighth goal – 'to build a global partnership for development' – aims to create the conditions necessary for achieving the other seven. With this goal the responsibility falls on the richer countries and the wider 'global community' to reduce debt, to give more and better aid, and to make trade fairer. One result of this has been the Global Campaign Against Poverty, which has brought people together from all over the world to lobby and demonstrate for trade justice and debt relief.

Focus on...
The United Nations

The United Nations officially came into existence on 24 October 1945. It is a global organisation with representatives from every country in the world. Its purpose is to maintain international peace and security, to build friendly relations between nations, to cooperate in solving international economic, social, cultural and humanitarian problems, and to promote human rights. UN members believe that lasting international peace is only possible if people everywhere have economic and social well-being, so the majority of its spending is on aid and development.

Disasters and Humanitarian Aid

While development aims to help countries improve their societies and economies over a long period of time, emergency aid is often needed when catastrophic events happen without warning. These may be natural disasters or events caused by people, such as wars and acts of terrorism. Many people argue that there should be more planning for disasters as part of long-term development work, particularly in areas where it is known that people are at risk.

A hazardous world

Most natural disasters are very sudden and extreme events that happen on the Earth's surface or in its atmosphere. They are either weather-related or geophysical in origin. Weather-related events include hurricanes, typhoons, cyclones and tornadoes, heavy rain that can cause flooding, or a lack of rain that causes drought. Geophysical events include earthquakes and volcanic activity, which can lead to tsunamis and landslides.

Natural disasters are not always as dramatic as this, though. Sometimes they can take place over a longer period of time, such as the temperature changes or fluctuations in surface waters in the Pacific Ocean known as El Niño and La Niña. These can have a huge effect on climates; in the long-term they can cause droughts or floods, and are responsible for deaths and damage to property on a large scale. Because the effects of these currents happen over a long period they receive less publicity, but they are just as devastating as hurricanes and earthquakes in terms of the damage and loss of life they can cause.

▲ Drought affects people's most precious assets – crops and animals. This is a dead donkey in the parched landscape of Darfur, an area also badly affected by conflict.

▲ It is estimated that 300,000 children are fighting in conflicts worldwide. Organisations like Save the Children help reunite child soldiers with their families and readjust to ordinary life.

Conflict and development

Conflicts are man-made disasters and they have become some of the biggest challenges to development, shattering people's lives and futures. Not only are lives lost but economic and social development are also badly affected. Factories are destroyed, production decreases, crops are not planted or harvested, roads are not built, and schools and hospitals close down. Money goes on buying guns and weapons instead of on development. Conflicts certainly cause poverty but they may also be caused by poverty.

Conflict also creates child soldiers and refugees. In 2002, 22 million people were internally displaced – refugees within their own country – and 13 million had to flee to other countries. The amount of aid needed in these kinds of situations is enormous and is required for many years after the conflict has ended.

Have your say

The global trade in arms and weapons has a massive impact on human quality of life and development. If governments are spending money on weapons they are not spending it on development.

- Is there a contradiction in a government spending money on the arms trade while also spending money on a foreign aid programme?
- Find out how much your country spends on arms and defence and on development, and then compare the two. What dilemmas does this raise?

A growing disaster

About 211 million people every year are affected by natural disasters. On average these disasters are responsible for the deaths of more than 60,000 people a year and affect at least a quarter of a billion people. The International Red Cross estimates that between 1994 and 1998 there were, on average, 428 disasters a year. But between 1999 and 2003 this shot up to an average of 707 disasters a year. The biggest rise was in weather-related disasters – possibly caused by climate change – and in LEDCs, which suffered an increase of 142 per cent. But natural disasters are happening more often and this figure looks set to increase.

The impact of disasters

It is estimated that 75 per cent of the world's population live in areas that have been affected at least once by either an earthquake, a tropical cyclone, by flooding or drought.

▼ Hurricane Katrina was one of the biggest disasters ever to hit the United States. More than 1,300 people died when the levees (walls built to prevent flooding) burst, allowing water to flood into the city of New Orleans and surrounding areas.

These are the figures we read about in the newspapers but we do not often hear how disasters affect people's lives for many years after the event. People lose their livelihoods, their homes and their sense of security and well-being. It can take many years for the situation to begin to return to normal.

Some countries are particularly vulnerable to disasters. Bangladesh and India are among the most disaster-prone countries in the world. A major cyclone hits the eastern shore of India every two to eight years, and huge areas of Bangladesh flood on a regular basis as a result of cyclones. The Caribbean islands, and increasingly the southern parts of the United States, are very vulnerable to hurricanes. The countries of East Africa – especially Eritrea, Ethiopia, Mozambique, Somalia, Sudan and Tanzania – are particularly vulnerable to drought and floods.

Focus on...
The Dandar earthquake

In 2005 a devastating earthquake hit Dandar, in north-west Pakistan. The town was hit by the full force of the earthquake. Every building was destroyed and many people were killed. In seconds people's lives were changed forever. They were left without homes and food. Even the road out of the town had disappeared. Emergency aid was supplied by several different aid organisations in the form of food and tents, but fresh, clean water was a problem. Many villagers had to walk more than 1.5 km across dangerous mountain paths and carry water back. After a year of waiting a pipeline has now been laid by Oxfam, and this brings clean water to the 4,000 people of Dandar.

▶ The 2005 Pakistan earthquake hit the country's capital Islamabad. Many buildings collapsed, killing and trapping thousands of people.

▲ Hygiene kits in blue buckets being prepared for distribution to people who have lost their homes as a result of the tsunami disaster in Sri Lanka in December 2004.

Disasters and the poor

Poor countries and poor people are disproportionately affected by disasters. They often do not have the money to pay for precautions against the effects of disasters and are more likely to live in areas that are higher-risk, such as on flood plains or steep slopes. Their houses are often unstable and poorly built. In 2003 an earthquake in Iran killed more than 40,000 people, mainly because their cheaply built housing of traditional mud brick and heavy roofs was not designed to withstand earthquakes.

After a disaster

The first 24 hours after a disaster are critical. The immediate priority is to save as many lives as possible. Countries from all over the world often offer help and expertise. After another earthquake in Iran in 2004 the Los

Angeles County Fire Department was one of many fire brigades from around the world, including the United Kingdom and South Africa, to send a rescue team. These rescue teams took specialist equipment and sniffer-dogs to help search for victims in the rubble of people's homes.

Injured people need to be taken to hospital, where doctors and nurses are needed to treat them. When disasters occur, the dead need to be buried as quickly as possible. Food, water and shelter are required immediately. Food and water may not be safe to eat or drink after a disaster. Medicines and vaccinations are needed as diseases can spread quickly where water is contaminated. People also need tents and blankets. Some aid organisations specialise in responding rapidly to disasters.

Inappropriate aid

Many countries are dependent on other countries to provide emergency aid. However, there has been some criticism of the aid provided in certain circumstances. The World Health Organisation (WHO) has suggested that some relief aid can be more harmful than helpful. After the Asian tsunami of December 2004 some of the medical aid sent included out-of-date drugs. It was also reported that some food packs containing pork were sent to Muslim communities. WHO has accused some small organisations of going to disaster areas just to gain publicity. They arrive too late and leave too early to be of any real or lasting assistance.

Have your say

Claude de Ville de Goyet from the International Red Cross says: 'People tend to consider that just because it is a European or an American [aid worker] that they can do better than a national would do in a disaster, and I'm sorry, but that is wrong.'

- Should people from the affected country be encouraged to take the lead in aid operations rather than people from other countries?
- Is it right for organisations from other countries to interfere in this way, even if they have more experience and resources?
- Do you agree or disagree with what Claude de Ville de Goyet is saying?

▼ A World Food Programme plane drops food at the Ararah camp, west of Darfur. The United Nations says that 50,000 people have been killed and one million displaced since fighting broke out in Darfur between the Sudanese government and two rebel groups in early 2003, sparking what has been called the world's worst humanitarian disaster.

▲ Cyclone shelters, such as this one in Bangladesh, provide safety for up to 400 people and can be the only thing left standing after a cyclone.

Reducing risk

A disaster can wipe out decades of development in a matter of hours. While there is little anyone can do about most disasters, some can be prevented and the devastating effects of many can be reduced. For example, in Japan, a country prone to earthquakes, buildings are built to withstand serious earthquake tremors. There are also special instruments called accelerometers placed along railway lines, which detect earthquakes as soon as they start. The electricity is immediately and automatically shut down and the trains are stopped. This technology is very expensive but undoubtedly saves lives.

Planning and predicting

In countries that cannot afford this kind of technology there are still measures that can be taken. Many aid programmes focus on developing effective early-warning systems and working with local people to carefully plan for disasters. People can be helped to build earthquake-proof houses on higher ground. Trees can be planted to stabilise the ground and prevent landslides.

In Bangladesh, aid agencies have helped build cyclone shelters. People have also been provided with radios and broadcasts are made in several different local dialects. When a flood is expected people are warned and have time to move into the shelters. All these measures can considerably reduce the impact of disasters.

Some kinds of disasters can be predicted. Technology such as satellite remote sensing

Focus on...
How natural are 'natural' disasters?

Some so-called 'natural' disasters are partly caused by humans. In 1965 the Koyna Reservoir in India was filled. Soon after this the area began to experience earth tremors that many believe were caused by the filling of the reservoir weakening a fault zone under the dam. In 1967 an earthquake measuring 6.5 on the Richter scale killed 177 people. The destruction of mangroves to make way for shrimp farms or because of rapid urban growth can increase the likelihood of damage from tsunamis, as the coast is left unprotected.

provides a method of monitoring worldwide agriculture and can help predict droughts and famines. In 2004, aid agencies and government departments in the United Kingdom and United States set up the Southern Africa Crisis Appeal. They could see from the early-warning systems and the failure of crops that famine would soon follow unless action was taken to help the people in the affected areas. The appeal was launched to avoid a full-scale humanitarian crisis. They hoped that in this way they could prevent a disaster rather than aid organisations having to respond to one.

Eyewitness

'We live very close to a cyclone shelter. We use it once or twice a year when we hear the grave danger signal. We have a transistor radio so I can always listen to what is happening with the weather patterns. Warnings of cyclones are pretty regular but it is not clear where they are going to strike until much later.'
Salma Katun, Bangladesh, quoted in *Dealing with Disasters*, Oxfam

▼ A farmer looks at the smoking land after trees have been burned to make way for farmland. Deforestation can lead to landslides and, ultimately, climate change.

Aid from Governments

The majority of aid in the world is given by governments, either through bilateral or multilateral aid. It is usually given as a grant or as a loan to another government, or through a multinational organisation to help them develop their economy or for a specific project. It is not unusual for countries to give aid to places in the same part of the world, or where there is a historical link. Japan, for example, devotes the majority of its aid spending to countries in Asia. France and the United Kingdom give most of their aid to their former colonies.

Bilateral aid

Bilateral aid is when one country's government gives aid to another country's government.

Bilateral aid accounts for nearly three-quarters of the total amount of aid given, and in 2003 this amounted to US$50 billion. A lot of bilateral aid goes on health and education programmes, or on large-scale construction projects like dams and transport systems.

Multilateral aid

Multilateral aid is aid that is channelled through organisations which, in themselves, are multinational. These include the World Health Organisation (WHO), the World Food Programme and the United Nations Educational, Scientific and Cultural Organisation (UNESCO) – which are part of the United Nations or other global organisations like the World Bank and

▼ The World Bank withdrew its funding for the Narmada Dam following a campaign of protest from those who would lose their land. Indian officials claim it is a 'necessary sacrifice' and many homes are now under water.

the International Monetary Fund (IMF). These organisations are usually governed by the countries that supply them with funds. The World Bank and the IMF have been criticised in the past for supporting projects that contribute to economic development – they have been the main institutions for providing loans to LEDCs – rather than concentrating enough on social and human development. However, the Millennium Development Goals (see page 14) mean that they may focus more directly on reducing poverty.

▲ Live 8 concerts took place in nine countries to publicise the need for action to be taken to help Africa at the G8 summit in 2005. This concert took place in Philadelphia, United States.

Focus on...
G8

In July 2005 the leaders of the eight major industrial democracies (France, the United States, the United Kingdom, Russia, Germany, Japan, Italy and Canada) met in Scotland to address continuing poverty in Africa by reducing and cancelling debt. While many people, including politicians and Bob Geldof, proclaimed the success of the G8 meeting, non-governmental organisations (see page 30) in particular felt the action did not go far enough towards meeting the needs of Africa and that the publicity was misleading. For example, it became apparent that the G8 had not in fact granted 100 per cent debt relief to 18 countries as first reported, but had only promised enough for them to write off their repayments for the next three years. Since the meeting many people feel that the promises made have been broken. Almost immediately Germany and Italy announced that they might not be able to meet the commitments they had made, and the IMF tried to overturn the deal it had made on debt relief.

Eyewitness

'This has been the most important summit there ever has been for Africa. There are no equivocations. Africa and the poor of that continent have got more from the last three days than they have ever got at any previous summit.'
Bob Geldof

'People must not be fooled by the celebrities, Africa got nothing.'
Demba Moussa Dembele of the Forum for African Alternatives

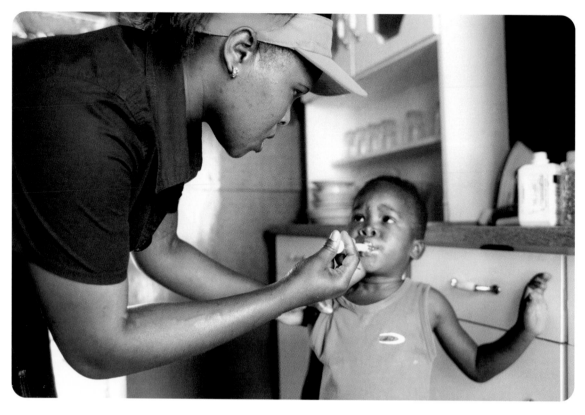

▲ In South Africa a three-year old boy is fed anti-retroviral medicines. This medicine is provided by Médecins Sans Frontières (Doctors Without Borders), an international medical aid agency. Whilst nearly everyone in MEDCs has access to HIV/AIDS treatment, less than 25 per cent of adults and less than 10 per cent of children have such access in LEDCs.

Tied aid

Government aid is often given with strings attached, so that it benefits the donor country. It may be that the donor country wants to gain some influence over the country that is receiving the aid, or it might want to increase its trade with the receiving country.

Aid with conditions attached is called 'tied aid'. An example of this is where a country receiving aid may have to buy a particular brand of tractors or anti-AIDS drugs from, say, the United States rather than cheaper drugs from South Africa or Brazil. Canada, the United States, Germany, Japan and France are all countries that insist that a major

proportion of their aid money is used to buy their own goods. Some people say this is giving with one hand and taking away with the other.

No strings attached

The most generous countries are also the ones that do not tie aid to their own products and services. These are the smaller aid-donor countries such as Sweden and Denmark, who do not have a history of colonialism and therefore feel no obligations to specific countries. Up to 90 per cent of aid from these countries is unconditional, or untied. Sweden, for example, gives aid for mine-clearing in Afghanistan and Iraq – countries with which it has no political or economic connection.

The arguments against tied aid seem to be winning over more countries. Much less aid now is tied than it was 25 years ago, and at the end of 2000 the United Kingdom announced it would be phasing it out altogether.

Aid as a lever

Aid is also used as a lever to control the actions of the receiving countries. In 2007 the European Union (EU) threatened to withdraw its aid to Nicaragua unless the country reversed a new law forbidding abortion under any circumstances. In 2003 the US government cut off funds to an HIV/AIDS programme in Africa because the US government objected to the use of condoms to combat HIV/AIDS in favour of advocating 'abstinence'.

Focus on...
Pergau dam

In 1991 work began on building a hydroelectric dam on the Pergau River in Malaysia to provide clean water in rural areas. The project was funded by the UK government to the tune of £59 million and the money was taken from its aid budget. But many people believed that the government had used aid money to 'sweeten' the Malaysian government who, at the same time, bought about £1 billion worth of arms and weapons from the United Kingdom. The case was so controversial that it was taken to the High Court, which ruled that the use of aid for this dam was illegal.

▼ Norwegian soldiers, part of the International Security Assistance Force (ISAF), load humanitarian aid for Afghanistan on to a German helicopter.

Who gives what?

In 1970, at the General Assembly of the United Nations, the governments of the world's richest countries promised they would donate 0.7 per cent of their gross national income (GNI) in aid. Yet, since then, nearly every wealthy country has failed to reach this obligation. Instead of 0.7 per cent, the amount of aid has averaged 0.2 to 0.4 per cent, some US$100 billion short.

However, recently five countries – Belgium, France, Ireland, Spain and the United Kingdom – have pledged to improve their aid budget to reach the UN target of 0.7 per cent of gross national income, at which point they would join Denmark, Luxembourg, the Netherlands, Norway and Sweden.

The biggest donors

Since 1992, and up until 2001, Japan was the largest donor of aid in terms of the total amount it gave. In 2001 the United States became the largest donor and in 2005, largely because of debt relief to Nigeria and Iraq and aid for victims of the Asian tsunami, US aid topped US$100 billion. However, in terms of a percentage of its GNI – 0.22 per cent – the

Official Development Assistance (2005)		
	ODA in US$ (millions)	ODA as % of GNI
Australia	1,666	0.25
Austria	678	0.52
Belgium	1,975	0.53
Canada	3,731	0.34
Denmark	2,107	0.81
Finland	897	0.47
France	10,059	0.47
Germany	9,915	0.35
Greece	535	0.24
Ireland	692	0.41
Italy	5,053	0.29
Japan	13,101	0.28
Luxembourg	264	0.87
Netherlands	5,131	0.82
New Zealand	274	0.27
Norway	2,775	0.93
Portugal	367	0.21
Spain	3,123	0.29
Sweden	3,280	0.92
Switzerland	1,771	0.44
United Kingdom	10,754	0.48
United States	27,457	0.22

(Source OECD, April 2006)

▲ This table shows the Official Development Assistance (ODA) of MEDCs in 2005.

▲ In Aceh, the area most badly affected by the 2004 tsunami, the target of rebuilding 100,000 homes by the end of 2006 was not met.

Focus on...
The Chad-Cameroon Oil Pipeline

In 2000 the World Bank funded the Chad-Cameroon Oil Pipeline project, despite objections from local groups in Chad that the money would go to a government with a record of human-rights abuses. A consortium of oil companies, led by ExxonMobil, paid the government US$25 million for signing the deal, which was spent on new weapons and the upgrading of politicians' offices. Most of the money from the oil revenues is now used to fund the conflict with neighbouring Sudan. In fact, less than two per cent of the US$3.7 billion paid by the World Bank has been used to help communities affected by the pipeline. Although the World Bank suspended payments for a while, it reinstated them after the Chad government promised that the money would go on development.

US contribution has almost always been lower than any other MEDC. Donations from individual Americans are more impressive, however, and in some years this has amounted to more than twice the US official foreign aid.

Aid going astray

Unfortunately, aid does not always reach its intended recipients. In conflict situations in particular there is the risk of aid being misappropriated by combatants rather than assisting the civilians for whom it was meant. In the chaos following a disaster aid can also sometimes go astray. Millions of pounds were donated after the 2004 tsunami but even in 2007 much of this had still not been spent.

Non-Governmental Organisations

The World Bank defines NGOs as 'private organisations that pursue activities to relieve suffering, promote the interests of the poor, protect the environment, provide basic social services, or undertake community development'. As their name implies, non-governmental organisations, which are also known as 'not-for-profit' and are often charities, operate independently from governments. However, many NGOs receive much of their funds from governmental sources. If all the NGOs in the world were put together, they would be the equivalent to the world's eighth-largest economy.

▲ A German Médecins Sans Frontières worker helps one of the youngest victims of flooding in Chokwe, Mozambique.

The origins of NGOs

Most NGOs started out as 'grassroots groups', where people came together when they felt something needed to be done about a particular situation. Oxfam, for example, started during the Second World War when Greece was the subject of a blockade. People there were going hungry, so a group of Quakers in Oxford in England formed the Oxford Committee for Famine Relief. They tried to persuade the British government to allow essential supplies through the blockade. Today Oxfam International is a group of 13 organisations working in more than 100 countries.

What do NGOs do?

Most NGOs, however, are quite small and are motivated by different factors. Some have a religious motivation, although this does not necessarily mean that they only work with people of the same faith. Some focus on a particular group of people such children or refugees. Others specialise in a specific service such as providing water or medical care. There are thousands of small NGOs that focus on individual communities in LEDCs

where they feel a link has been established with their own communities.

NGOs are directly involved in development and focus more on the social and human side than multilateral agencies and governments tend to. They see their role as empowering people to have more say over their own lives, to provide welfare services, to lobby decision-makers to take account of the poor (increasingly in areas such as arms controls and trade), and to build up the ability of local organisations in their work on development. Most NGOs would say that they try to tackle the root causes of poverty.

Focus on...
CARE

CARE is one of the largest NGOs in the United States. It focuses on working with poor women because it believes that by helping women it will help whole families and entire communities to develop. In 2005 CARE spent more than US$515 million on its programme, raised from individuals, corporations, foundations, US government agencies, the European Union and the United Nations.

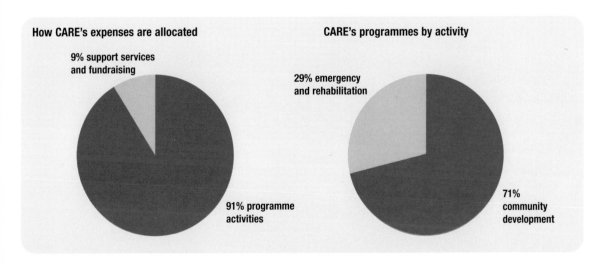

How CARE's expenses are allocated

9% support services and fundraising

91% programme activities

CARE's programmes by activity

29% emergency and rehabilitation

71% community development

Grassroots development

Outsiders cannot 'do' development to people. Local people have to drive it at their own pace if it is to have any lasting impact. Most NGOs take this into account in their work. They spend time talking with local people to help them develop their own understanding and have their own voice about how they think their lives could be improved. Most NGOs work through local organisations, known as 'partners', to achieve this, and more and more NGOs are based in LEDCs.

NGO dilemmas

Dealing with humanitarian situations thrown up by conflicts is a key challenge for some of the largest NGOs. In the case of the war in Iraq, for example, NGOs have had to distance themselves in the eyes of the Iraqis from the US and British forces. In 2003 an attack on the headquarters of the Red Cross in Baghdad showed how dangerous and difficult it can be for them to continue with their work in these circumstances. In Darfur in southern Sudan, members of NGOs have

▼ The aftermath of the massive car-bomb attack on the headquarters of the Red Cross in Baghdad, Iraq, on 27 October 2003. The attack killed at least 10 people.

Eyewitness

The use of celebrities by NGOs has become a controversial issue.

'It's bad enough having to accommodate celebrities and their entourage in the aftermath of every major humanitarian disaster, but when most people think of the UN now they think of Angelina Jolie on a crusade, not the work that goes on in the field after humanitarian disasters or on a long-term preventative level.'
UNICEF officer in New Delhi, quoted in
The Observer, 26 November 2006

▲ Thousands of demonstrators gathered in Edinburgh on 2 July 2005 to take part in the Make Poverty History rally, urging leaders of the G8 nations to help defeat global poverty.

been kidnapped, assaulted and robbed by government forces and militias on a regular basis. Many NGOs have withdrawn personnel from the worst-affected areas. In Iraq many western NGOs find they can now only work through partner organisations.

Funding and publicising work

Some NGO funds come from government grants and businesses but most rely on voluntary contributions from the public. This money is raised in a variety of ways, from street collections to television 'telethons' and telephoning people at home.

The areas of aid and development have become highly competitive. Increasing numbers of NGOs are fighting for the funds available and will go to great lengths to raise their profile. The larger NGOs now have public-relations departments that are responsible for promoting their organisation and the work they do. Some NGOs have been criticised for exaggerating the seriousness of some situations in order to raise more funds, although this is not normally the case.

Focus on...
Make Poverty History

Make Poverty History is a coalition of about 450 NGOs. It started in 2005 and claims it is the biggest-ever anti-poverty movement, achieving support from a huge range of people around the world. Following its publicity success at the 2005 G8 summit at Gleneagles, in 2007 it asked people to email the German chancellor, Angela Merkel, who held the presidency of the EU, asking her to put poverty at the top of the agenda. MPH has been spectacularly successful at publicising its cause – particularly through the Live 8 concerts – but has not always achieved what it has set out to do.

Volunteering

Out of concern for the welfare of others and a sense of outrage at the injustices that exist in the world, many people engage in activities and actions of their own. President Kennedy established the Peace Corps in the United States, and in the United Kingdom there is Voluntary Service Overseas (VSO). These schemes provide opportunities for people to work in LEDCs, using and sharing their skills to fight poverty.

Philanthropy

Many people who have been lucky enough to make their fortunes often feel the need to give something back. Bill Gates, who started Microsoft, has set up a fund and donated US$800 million to a worldwide infant vaccination programme. George Soros, who made a fortune by speculating on the stock market, has given away millions of dollars, including US$50 million to the Jeffrey Sachs Millennium Promise to eradicate extreme poverty in Africa.

On a much smaller scale there are now websites that enable individuals and companies to find and support grassroots projects around the world. This means people can see exactly where their money is going and how it is being used.

Sending money home

Sending money home to families in LEDCs plays a vital role in helping to tackle poverty. A survey in the United Kingdom found that 38 per cent of ethnic-minority households

▼ UN Children's Education fund director Ann Veneman and economist Jeffrey Sachs visit development projects focusing on education in Kenya.

▲ A volunteer from the UK-based organisation VSO working in a centre for street children in Tanzania.

sent on average £878 home, mainly to Nigeria, India, Pakistan and Ghana. Ghana receives 10 to 15 per cent of its national income from remittances sent from around the world, compared to around three per cent from foreign investment. It is estimated that in 2004, Kenyans working abroad remitted about US$464 million, which was about twice the amount of aid Kenya received. Remittances from the United States are particularly important to Latin America and the Caribbean where, it is estimated, three-quarters of remittances received come from the United States.

In 2005, officially recorded remittances worldwide exceeded US$232 billion, with LEDCs receiving US$167 billion of this – more than twice the level of development aid from all sources. Remittances sent through informal channels could add another 50 per cent to the official estimate.

Focus on...
Millennium Villages

The Bugesera District in Rwanda was one of the worst-hit areas during the 1994 genocide. In Bugesera today there is a series of Millennium Villages, which are empowered to meet the Millennium Development Goals through integrated, holistic development. This means that all areas are focused on development, including health, food production, education, access to clean water and other essential requirements. There have already been many successes: malaria has been reduced, maternal and child mortality rates are improving, and agricultural produce has tripled. In addition to this, the programme aims to involve local people in making decisions about what is needed and how their village will develop.

Many large transnational companies have made fat profits from their dealings with LEDCs. Increasingly, shareholders and holding companies are calling these transnationals to account for their investments.

Challenges for Aid and Development

Aid has become a huge global business, but it faces big challenges. People in many countries still live in poverty despite the vast amounts of money that have been spent on aid in the last few decades, raising big questions about its effectiveness. Unfortunately the amount of aid given is not an indication of its success. The quality of aid has been much criticised, but people are now asking whether aid in itself will ever be enough and whether solutions to world poverty might lie elsewhere. Debt, unfair trading practices and conflict continue to undermine aid programmes and the development of many countries. As well as this, the possible consequences of climate change could spell disaster for the poor.

Corruption

Many critics of aid argue that it does not reach the poor, as it is misappropriated by corrupt officials both in MEDCs and in LEDCs. Some notorious dictators, such as Mobutu in Zaire and Ferdinand Marcos in the Philippines, have stolen millions of dollars in aid money despite the poverty of their countries. But aid has also sometimes

▲ Local volunteers in Sri Lanka, displaced by the 2004 tsunami, are trained in hygiene education.

Eyewitness

'We try to save lives in the short-term so that people have the chance of a long-term future. Our role is to keep people alive and enable them to get back on their feet, knowing and demanding that the root cause of the crisis must be addressed in a different way.'
The UK Disasters Emergency Committee Annual Review, 2002

'Billions of pounds worth of aid has poured into Africa in the past fifty years. I suggest as a starting point that the development of peoples, of societies, can only be done by those people themselves. It cannot be done by outsiders.'
Richard Dowden, Director of the Royal African Society, in a speech made in 2004

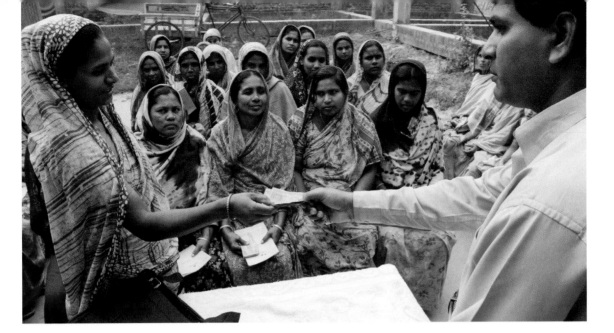

▲ A woman borrows money from the Grameen Bank at the weekly meeting.

been used by donor countries to control and influence other countries, or to prop up dictators just because they were 'on the right side'.

Balancing the benefits

Another challenge for aid is to ensure it does not undermine local economies. Even food aid, which on the surface seems like the obvious solution to hunger, can contribute to an increase in poverty. The sudden availability of quantities of food can under-sell local farmers, making it impossible for them to sell their produce. This can ultimately affect the whole economy of a poor country.

Good models for development?

Some people look to China and India as good models of how countries can develop. Both these countries are experiencing rapid economic development. Together they make up about one-third of the world's population, and incomes are rising rapidly. Millions have been taken out of poverty. However, both China and India are now faced with the

Focus on...
The Grameen Bank

The Grameen Bank is a microfinance organisation in Bangladesh. It provides credit for poor people, 97 per cent of whom are women. They are able to take out small loans without providing any collateral, allowing them to set up small businesses. As soon as they have repaid a loan they can take out another. The bank has been hugely successful at lifting people out of poverty. In 2006 the bank and its founder, Muhammad Yunus, were awarded the Nobel Peace Prize. Yunus believes that credit is a human right. He says, 'Grameen believes that charity is not an answer to poverty. It only helps poverty to continue. It creates dependency and takes away an individual's initiative to break through the wall of poverty.'

problems that often come with development – particularly increasing levels of pollution. China especially, with its dependency on coal as a fuel and the rise in car ownership, is suffering from dangerously high levels of air and water pollution. There are other issues, too. When development occurs at such a breakneck speed, it can leave many people still in poverty, alienated from the benefits of economic progress.

Debt as a cause of poverty

In the 1980s the president of Tanzania, Julius Nyere asked, 'Should we really let our children starve so that we can pay our debts?' Every day, sub-Saharan Africa spends £26 million on paying back debts to governments, banks and global organisations such as the World Bank and the International Monetary Fund.

The IMF and World Bank introduced what they called structural adjustment policies, which resulted in cutbacks in spending on healthcare, education and other vital social services. The idea was that such policies would enable these countries to pay off their loans. In addition, the governments of LEDCs are required to open their economies to compete with one another and with more powerful and established industrialised nations.

Debt forgiveness

After decades of pressure from NGOs and campaigners, some world leaders called for debt forgiveness (cancelling or reducing the amount of debt owed by certain countries) by the World Bank, IMF and African Development Bank – for around 23 countries whose regimes are considered sufficiently pro-western and pro-market oriented. Without this kind of debt relief it is highly unlikely that the Millennium Development Goals will be achieved.

Some western nations – France and Germany in particular – were uncomfortable about offering this kind of debt forgiveness. This was not because they did not want poor countries to benefit, but because they thought it was a bad idea to reward what

▲ The World Bank was set up to support development projects and provide loans to LEDCs.

Have your say

It is estimated that debt cancellation in Nicaragua would make US$350 million a year available to spend on providing an education for thousands of children by building over 1,000 classrooms and 350 schools; 400 health centres and hospitals could be updated, improving healthcare for 900,000 poor people. It could also provide clean water for 450,000 people in rural areas.

• Should there be strings attached to debt relief for Nicaragua?
• What arguments might there be for not cancelling the debt?
• What alternative measures could be taken to help Nicaragua out of its current problems?

▲ A woman volunteer teacher shows a man how to print letters on a blackboard as part of the Nicaraguan Literacy Campaign.

they saw in many cases as severe financial mismanagement. They worried that a country that failed to pay off its debts and had them removed may still find it hard to get loans in the future, as they would still be considered a credit risk. Under the Marshall Plan, grants were given rather than loans. Some people, including the economist Jeffrey Sachs, a special adviser to the United Nations, think that it would be a good idea to have a similar system and 'emulate that wisdom today'.

Focus on...
Debt vultures

A 'vulture fund' is a company that buys up the debts of indebted countries cheaply and then sues through the courts for the original value of the debt, plus interest. In 1999, Donegal International, part-owned by US-based Debt Advisory International, bought a debt owed by Zambia – originally worth US$15 million – for only US$3.3 million. It then sued Zambia for the full amount, plus interest and costs – a total of over US$40 million. This amount is equal to the value of all the aid received by Zambia in 2006. In 2007, a court ruled that by law Donegal were entitled to receive something from Zambia, but only about half the amount they were claiming.

Prosperity through trade

Globalisation in trade has brought the world closer together but, at the same time, created greater inequalities. It is through trade that countries become richer and international trade usually represents a significant share of gross domestic income. In Britain, in the nineteenth century, trade provided the resources for the Industrial Revolution and the country developed and flourished. In those times the terms of trading were decided on between two nations but were based on a belief in free trade, where goods and services between countries flows unhindered.

▲ The sale and export of goods has improved the economies of many countries.

Disadvantaging the poor

After the Second World War measures were brought in to regulate trade on a more global scale. The General Agreement on Tariffs and Trade (GATT) and, subsequently, the World Trade Organisation (WTO), introduced new terms to create a global trade structure with the removal or reduction of barriers. For many countries, lowering barriers was a viable policy. No MEDC in the past has been able to industrialise without protection and help from its government for critical industries – something that is now being denied LEDCs.

In fact, the current global terms of trade are actively leading to the underdevelopment of many of the world's poorest countries. Under global trading rules, European, American and Japanese farmers receive subsidies that allow them to produce more food and sell it more cheaply. This has led to 'food dumping' on developing world markets. These unrestricted food imports, in particular to LEDCs, destroy local economies and livelihoods. They make local farmers' produce too expensive. Powerful interests in the richer countries are reluctant to drop measures that protect their own markets.

Fair trade

In view of the problems with trade between richer and poorer countries interest has grown in alternative trade, also known as ethical or fair trade. Under alternative trade, producers – mainly farmers – are guaranteed a price for their produce that gives them a decent return. The Fairtrade Foundation says that 'Fairtrade focuses on ensuring that farmers in developing countries receive an agreed and stable price for the crops they grow, as well as an additional Fairtrade premium to invest in social projects or business development programmes.'

However, fair trade is not without its critics. Many people argue that unless the trading relationship between rich and poor countries is improved, all the benefits of aid will be worth nothing. It is trade, they say, that will lead to methods of production that will lift people out of poverty in a sustainable way. They argue that trade is worth 20 times as much as aid.

Have your say

Steve Daley who works with the charity Worldwrite says that fair trade is more about 'flattering Western shoppers' – making consumers feel better because they are helping someone who is poor. He argues that fair trade is just a drop in the ocean because it only provides a small increase in the farmer's wage. What is needed is for poor agricultural communities to be completely modernised.

• Do you think you as an individual have any responsibility for poverty?
• What do you think you can do about it?

▼ In Haiti, one of the poorest countries in the world, coffee farmers are helped by a local cooperative to process and market their coffee beans. These women are carrying baskets of coffee beans to a fair-trade market.

The Great Debate

Everyone agrees that something should be done about poverty, but there is much debate about the best way to tackle it and how effective aid is.

Critics of aid say that it has not been used well:

● They argue that much of aid has been used for political purposes rather than helping the poor.

● It has gone to war-torn and politically unstable countries where in many cases it has not reached those people who needed it most.

● It has gone to dictators and corrupt regimes with little interest in the welfare of their people.

● The biggest critics even say that it keeps people poor and can actually hinder development.

● They say that rather than aid what is needed are fundamental, sustainable changes to the world's trading systems, to enable poor countries to develop and be able to stand on their own.

'Too much of the $300 million in aid to Africa since 1980 has vanished into a sinkhole of fraud, malfeasance and waste.'
Sharon LaFraniere, *New York Times*, July 2005

Those who advocate aid think that it is an essential tool for helping people:

● They highlight the fact that aid can actually save people's lives, especially in emergency situations, through providing essential supplies of food and water, for example.

● They use examples of aid systems such as the Grameen Bank to show that aid can fundamentally change and improve people's lives, especially by helping them to help themselves.

● They argue that although there may have been problems in the past, major changes have taken place and aid is now targeted more carefully.

● Aid is increasingly going to countries with better human rights and accountability.

'...Reality is broadly the opposite of current popular beliefs. Aid has not been wasted: it has kept African economies afloat through disturbed times.'
Paul Collier, 'What Can We Expect From More Aid to Africa?' May 2006

Facts and Figures

- More than 83 aid workers were killed in Iraq between 2003 and 2007, the highest number of aid workers killed in any one country.

- Donor governments promised to spend 0.7 per cent of GNI on Official Development Assistance at the UN General Assembly in 1970.

- In 2005 Iraq was the top recipient of Official Development Assistance and received US$12,924 million.

- Remittances sent by Mexicans living and working in the United States account for 1.5 per cent of Mexico's national income total.

- More than one million people have received HIV/AIDS drugs, 2.8 million have been treated for tuberculosis and around 30 million families have received bed nets through the efforts of the Global Fund to Fight AIDS, Tuberculosis and Malaria.

- Half the world – nearly three billion people – lives on less than two dollars a day.

- The country with the highest infant mortality rate is Angola, with 185.36 deaths per 1,000 live births. The country with the lowest is Singapore, with 2.28 deaths.

- From 1998–2001 the United States, the United Kingdom and France earned more income from arms sales to LEDCs than they gave in aid.

- Every day the poorest countries in the world transfer US$100 million to the richest countries in debt repayments.

- The richest fifth of the world's people consumes 86 per cent of all goods and services, while the poorest fifth consumes just 1.3 per cent.

- Of the 4.4 billion people in LEDCs, nearly three-fifths lack access to safe sewers, a third have no access to clean water, a quarter do not have adequate housing and a fifth have no access to modern health services of any kind.

- The cost of providing basic healthcare and nutrition for everyone in the world would be less than that spent on pet food in Europe and the United States.

- The richest 20 per cent of the world's people account for 86 per cent of the world's GDP while the poorest 20 per cent of people have just one per cent of the GDP.

- The United Nations estimates that more than 130,000 children in Africa are dying every week because of debt.

Further Information

Books

How to Be A Fundraising Champion: A practical manual for young activists by Michael Norton (Community Links, 2004)

Poverty (Planet Under Pressure) by Clive Gifford and Paul Mason (Raintree, 2006)

Sustainable Human Development by Peace Child International (Evans Brothers, 2003)

The No-Nonsense Guide to Fair Trade by David Ransom (New Internationalist, 2001)

The No-Nonsense Guide to Globalization by Wayne Ellwood and John McMurty (New Internationalist, 2001)

The Red Cross Movement (World Watch) by Jane Bingham (Hodder Children's Books, 2003)

UNICEF (World Watch) by Steven Maddocks (Hodder Children's Books, 2003)

Websites

http://www.grameen-info.org/
The website of the Grameen Bank, explaining how the bank developed and offering case studies.

http://www.msf.org/
Médecins Sans Frontières: the website of the humanitarian medical aid agency.

http://www.oxfam.org/
Oxfam International's website, which has a wide range of information about aid, development and campaigning.

http://www.bized.co.uk/virtual/dc/
The Virtual Developing Country website explores a number of development issues using a case-study approach.

http://www.j8summit.com/
J8, an education programme providing information about issues on the G8 agenda, with fact sheets and lesson plans.

http://www.globaleye.org.uk/secondary_autumn04/eyeon/coffeetrade.html
The Global Eye site, with activities on coffee production in Colombia.

Teaching resources

www.leedsdec.org.uk
Can debt relief help the world's poor? This website uses case studies from Senegal, Nicaragua and South Africa, and contrasts micro-credit schemes with international lender projects.

www.oxfam.org.uk/coolplanet
Change the world in eight steps. This is a set of posers and activities for 7–14 year-olds investigating the UN Millennium Development Goals.

http://www.oxfam.org.uk/education/resources/milking.it/milkingit
A website for teachers, with classroom activities that compare the lives of dairy farmers in Wales and Jamaica, demonstrating how they are both affected by trade issues.

Looking Behind the Logo: the Global Supply Chain in the Sportswear Industry A book published by Oxfam (2007), giving tips on making the idea of the global supply chain relevant to children.

Dealing with Disasters: Teaching About Disasters and Development An Oxfam book (2000) looking at the causes and effects of natural disasters.

The Trading Game: How Trade Works A book published by Christian Aid – a simulation designed to introduce students to the realities of trade and how it can affect the prosperity of a country.

Glossary

beneficiary someone who receives funds or aid.

bilateral aid aid given from one country to another.

cash crops crops such as coffee or tea that are grown for direct sale and export rather than for food.

colonies countries that were taken over and ruled by another.

debt money owed by a person, business or country to another.

deforestation the process of cutting down trees and clearing forests.

development a process of change for the better – usually the economy grows, standards of living rise, quality of life improves, wealth is shared more evenly and more people take part in decision-making.

donor a person, organisation or country that gives money, goods or some other kind of help to others.

drought an extended period of unusually low rainfall, causing water shortages and crop damage.

emergency assistance aid given to people (e.g. refugees) in countries suffering from natural disasters, wars or other major upheavals.

ethnic minority a group of people whose origins are different from the majority of the total population.

famine an extreme shortage of food caused by poor harvests or by food supplies being cut off or destroyed during wars or natural disasters.

G8 the group of the world's most powerful countries: Canada, France, Germany, Italy, Japan, Russia, the United Kingdom and United States.

geophysical relating to the Earth and the environment.

grassroots organisation an organisation driven by members of the local community.

Gross National Income the total value of goods and services produced within a country, together with its income from other countries minus similar payments made to other countries.

humanitarian concerned with human welfare and well-being.

import to buy goods and products from another country.

infrastructure basic facilities and services needed for the functioning of a community, such as roads, water, electricity and schools.

interdependence when different things depend on each other e.g. with increasing globalisation countries now often depend on one another.

international trade buying or selling items or services between countries.

less economically developed country (LEDC) one of the poorer countries of the world. LEDCs include all of Africa, Asia (except Japan), Latin America and the Caribbean, and Melanesia, Micronesia and Polynesia.

malaria a disease caused by being bitten by a mosquito, which can be fatal.

more economically developed country (MEDC) one of the richer countries of the world. MEDCs include all of Europe, North America, Australia, New Zealand and Japan.

multilateral aid aid channelled through international organisations such as the UN agencies and the World Bank.

non-aligned not allied with any other nation or bloc – neutral.

non-governmental organisation (NGO) any organisation that is neither run by the state nor makes a profit. Charities are NGOs.

official development grants and loans at concessional rates to promote economic development and welfare. Military aid and grants from NGOs are not counted as official development.

plantations specialised farms growing one particular crop often for foreign markets e.g. tea, coffee, rubber.

Quakers a religious sect who refer to themselves as the Society of Friends.

quality of life more than just the material things of life, e.g. security, healthcare, education, friends, social activity, basic rights.

refugee someone who flees in search of refuge from war, political oppression or religious persecution.

remittances money sent home to family and friends by people from LEDCs living in the MEDCs.

self-sufficient an individual or country that is able to provide for itself.

standard of living a level of material comfort measured by the goods and services available to an individual or group.

structural adjustment a term used to describe the policy changes imposed by the IMF and the World Bank on LEDCs for getting new loans or obtaining lower interest rates on existing loans.

sub-Saharan Africa the region of Africa south of the Sahara desert.

tariff a duty or tax imposed by a government on imported or exported goods.

transnational company a company that operates in markets that cut across national borders.

tuberculosis an infectious disease of the lungs.

vaccination an inoculation in order to protect against a particular disease.

welfare the health and happiness of people.

Index